Think on These Things

Think
on These Things

*"As we have borne the image of
the earthy, we shall also bear the
image of the heavenly."*

I Cor. 15, 42

*"We all, with open face, behold-
ing as in a glass the glory of the
Lord, are changed into the same
image from glory to glory, even
as by the spirit of the Lord."*

II Cor. 3.18

1921
STAR-NEWS PUBLISHING COMPANY
PASADENA, CALIFORNIA

Think on These Things

This book is made up chiefly of communications from the invisible realms of life; and by that phrase I mean not some strange and distant sphere, but a world that lies all about us, interpenetrating and intermingling with our common, every-day life, though ordinarily we are unconscious of its existence.

In one way and another it befalls, from time to time, that a man or a woman is aware of something like the quickening of a new sense; when that which has hitherto been invisible, intangible, inaudible, enters the waking consciousness and makes itself known as real, vital, and of supreme importance. So it comes about that there are some of us for whom it is no longer possible to think of that "other world" as wholly separate from our present selves; no longer possible to think of Death as a blank, impenetrable curtain that shuts us off from all knowledge of those who once gave significance and purpose to our lives.

In my own case it was not until I went down to face the very blackness of Death, when it seemed that my eyes could never weep again or my ears hearken to any song of Life, that the Spirit touched me, the inner sense awoke, and I received the assurance of things pure, lovely, and of good report.

Perhaps it is not possible to impart this assurance to others who have not had such direct experience, but as we can darken one another's lives by the shadow of our doubts, fears, and unbelief, so surely we may hope to share in some measure the light that comes from Love revealed beyond the confines of our day and night.

The messages herein recorded were received by me through so-called automatic writing. That is, they were written by a pencil held in my hand, but the process of writing and the words written were as detached from my volition as the clicking of a telegraphic instrument that brings a message from another continent.

It is not my purpose here to offer a treatise on psychical research or to enter upon a discussion of the scientific evidence for survival. A detailed account of the mystic experience crowded into one year of my life would fill a large volume. The more striking evidences of identity, amounting in my mind to indisputable proof, which were furnished me at an early stage in the communications have been laid before the American Society for Psychical Research and are now in their hands for publication in the Journal of the Society.

By the word of many witnesses Truth is established. A multitude, past and present, have testified to the reality of life after death and to the possibility of communication between the realms visible and invisible. It is my belief that much can be learned by giving more careful attention to the content of the messages received.

I can do no more now than publish a few fragments of all that came to me. As for their genuineness as communications received in the manner I shall describe and for the truth of such statements as I shall make in regard to them I can only say that I, who write these words, believe in the immortality of the Spirit, I believe that the messages came, as purported, from my Beloved, and with all that I know and hope for of love, human and divine, at stake, I shall not bear false witness.

The earliest message in writing came to me about fifteen months after the sudden death of my husband, in response to experiments made in mingled scepticism and longing. The evidence of identity to which I have referred consisted of three incidents which were quite unknown to me. They had taken place, one about four months previous to my husband's death, the others nearly two years before, and two thousand miles from the scene of the communications. Each incident was known to but one living person—the same one for two of the incidents—and from these two persons I obtained detailed and exact confirmation of all that had been told me, even to the words spoken on each occasion. In one case I was able, by skillful questioning, to elicit this confirmation without giving, on my part, a single detail of the incident which I wished to have recalled.

This was evidence of a nature which should have some standing even in a court of law. Of evidence poignantly convincing to me but not susceptible of corroboration by others, there was abundance.

The communications increased in frequency and volume during a period of several months until they occupied my time for many hours every day. At the end of a year they had diminished to a few lines at irregular intervals; after that they almost ceased and no attempts, desire, or prayers of mine have availed to bring back the earlier fulness and freedom.

While I was in the midst of this daily experience I set down a carefully accurate account of the manner of the writing and of my impressions at the time. The following paragraphs are quoted from that description, which was written by me late in the fall of 1919.

"I have never been in trance or any state approaching trance. I am in full waking consciousness and in possession of all my faculties. . . . Yet my hand is controlled. One cannot prove this to the sceptical, but the fact remains to the one who knows, conclusive—unescapable. There is something felt in the hand and arm, a potent force unknown to the body hitherto. One does not know what the hand is about to do. It writes sometimes with a light, flying touch, sometimes with great vigor and assertion and hard bearing-down. It twitches about, flourishes, gesticulates with the pencil; insists upon arbitrary things such as writing the words in a column, one under the other down the page; or printing, sometimes in tiny letters, sometimes in large capitals. I do not often oppose its will for I want the message, but I have had the pencil refuse to move when I have purposely tried to change a word that was being written.

I have never written with a pencil at any other time in my life. I learned to write with a No. 1 Spencerian pen and I have never used anything else except for the purpose of these communications, which have to be taken down with pencil because they come with a speed and continuity which preclude stopping to dip pen in ink. At first the words were all run together and the pencil never lifted except to pass from one sheet to the next, but for some time now the words have been detached and well spaced. T's are never crossed nor i's dotted.

There are times when the control is as firm and unmistakable as if some strong guiding hand were laid over my own—more than that, for the control is felt throughout the muscles of the arm. At other times I am conscious, at first, of hardly more than a blind impulse to write, not knowing what the first stroke will be. In early days at such times I would pause, perhaps thinking, 'There is no power,' and then would come the plaintive request, 'Please move the pencil for me,' and as I obeyed the words would continue to shape themselves with increasing clearness and speed.

Sometimes I seem to hear the words before they are written, as if some one were dictating and keeping two or three words ahead of me all the time. . . . Even so I have many times had another word substituted, in the instant of writing, for the one I was too sure of—done, too, with a twitch of the pencil that seemed to say, 'So you think you know just what I am going to do? Well, I'll show you that you don't.' At other times the matter has been all strange, unknown, unguessed, and with a quality of suspense which has kept me almost breathless from word to word.

The communications might be separated into three classes. One that is, as I have said, like something written from dictation, and here there is more formality of expression than at other times, as if the matter had been prepared or thought out in advance. The second and largest class would comprise those writings that are of the nature of a conversation. My part, whether question, answer, or comment, was not spoken but was clearly formulated in thought. In the earlier records these conversations appear as monologues; later I formed the habit of going over the writing as soon as it was completed and jotting down my own part in the conversation as well as I could remember it. In the third class I seemed to find myself writing down the *thoughts* of another. These always came with the utmost rapidity and I was compelled to write at something close to telegrapher's speed.

It appeared that at such times F. did not always know, even, that I was writing, and thus it chanced that I overheard, as it were, some of the most intimate self-searchings and self-revealings—such things as are not spoken even between the nearest and dearest. After one or two dramatic episodes when I was "discovered" and made to feel that I had stolen in, unaware, to a secret place, I learned to announce my presence more plainly. But it seemed that sometimes the thoughts ran wild and were beyond control, for the hurried words would come—they always seemed to me like a cry—'Don't let me say that'! Of course the only way I could prevent the 'saying' was to stop writing, with a mind full of awe and wonder at the strange conditions that seemed to enable me to listen, if I chose, to the inmost thoughts of one who had gone beyond sight or touch."

This was a phase that soon passed and as these communications were especially intimate and personal they are only slightly represented in the pages that follow.

It hardly needs to be said that the companionship between F. and myself had been unusually close. We had travelled much, read much, thought and talked much. We shared the love of Nature, books, and music. Neither of us was of a religious temperament. F. was a worldly agnostic; I used to call myself "an emancipated Puritan," but the emancipation went so far that it left me adrift with very little fixity of belief in anything.

It was only in the two years just preceding F.'s death that some study of Eastern teachings had brought to both of us belief in the persistence of conscious individuality after death. We accepted this, as we accepted the idea of reincarnation, partly because it suddenly appeared reasonable to us, but more, I think, because we felt the crying need in ourselves of some hint of completion in the curious pattern of our lives. There was that in the twisting, weaving threads, even for the little space that we could see, that told of more than chance behind the veil of the past and that demanded of the future something more than the shears of Atropos.

On the subject of our reading I should say that we had touched upon Psychical Research, without going into it deeply. We had together read Sir Oliver Lodge's *Raymond* and this book did, for me, the important work of breaking down much of my life-long prejudice against spiritualism. (I have never known a medium or attended a seance.) During the year of my communicating I read several books dealing with the subject in a general way but none that contained verbatim messages—unless I should except Lodge's *Survival of Man*. In the summer of 1920 I turned my attention to the recent literature of communications and was amazed to find how many such books had been published while I was "writing."

Coming down now to the present book: the selections I give here from the messages received by me are nearly all in chronological order and date from August, 1919, to March, 1920, with a very few of later date added. I had been writing in this way for four months prior to August, but the earlier communications were for the most part intensely personal; a few were confused or incoherent; others were fantastic; in some there seemed to be an intrusion of alien personalities. F. often spoke of himself as in darkness or fog, although from the first this condition seemed to alternate with one in which perception was almost blinded by a radiance of spiritual light.

I have frankly chosen for this little book such messages as would illustrate, first the personal characteristics that were so strong in all the early and middle period of the communicating, and later, the steady dawning of a spiritual purpose which seems, at last, to have carried my Beloved into regions where I may not follow while I am still weighted to earth by this garment of the flesh.

In respect to the editing which these messages have received, I wish to be explicit. These are, avowedly, extracts. Very few communications are given in their entirety. The more important omissions are indicated by dots; in some instances I have joined the portions retained, where the continuity of sense allowed this to be done, and in a few cases I have written in a single connecting word. These omissions have been mainly in the interest of condensation: in no case has the sense of the original been changed.

The script, to use the technical expression, is almost devoid of punctuation; occasionally a period, very rarely an interrogation point or marks of quotation—that is all. So I have punctuated in more or less orthodox fashion.

Beyond this I have not in any way altered or added to what was given me.

The copied page is, however, sadly dull and inexpressive beside the original, with its varying thought and emotion reflected in many changes, sometimes subtle and sometimes exceedingly obvious, in the size and character of the writing. An exclamation point is but a poor substitute for the sudden soaring that came with the thought of greatness or beauty and inscribed itself in big, round letters that covered four or five spaces of my ruled paper!

It is far from my desire to be dogmatic in regard to anything contained in the following pages. We may be sure that so long as there is individuality there is not omni-science, and I hope there are many who will rejoice, as I do, at every fresh evidence of the Many Mansions in Our Father's house, with infinite love and compassion abiding over all.

I wish only that this may be taken for what it is—the authentic, though partial, record of a genuine experience; and I would ask those who are given to thinking in terms of the "subconscious," to be very sure that that word is a true symbol representing an idea in their minds, not merely an empty phrase used to obviate the necessity for a definite idea.

It may so easily turn out that the "subconscious" is no other than the imperishable Soul, and wiser than we dream!

"For within you is the light of the world, the only light that can be shed upon the Path."

NOTE—I have enclosed in parentheses the occasional words which represent my part in the "conversation" when the communication took place.

Square brackets are used to enclose any later editorial comment, after the usual custom.

I have retained unaltered the familiar name which F. had given me and which he used freely throughout the communications as he had always done in the earth-life.

COMMUNICATIONS

... You must not ask questions for they confuse the vibrations. It is all vibrations, Harrie, but I can't explain how the process is carried on. I only know that when I think you hear what I think....

You and I both have the faculty of seeing each other's dream pictures as clearly as if they were our own.... When you think of beauty you do create it here and I see it. You are really one of the most idealistic persons I ever knew, Harrie. I never half knew you when we were on earth. You have shown me sides of your nature that I never suspected. You say neither did you, but they were there or they could not come out now.

Surely we must have life together on our own plane of love and beauty—beautiful things, such as flowers, music, stars, and the sea!

(The writing always grows so big when you speak of the sea!)

Yes, the sea sends me up, but I will not go up now for I mean to write while I can.... You know my imagination runs away with me still; yes, just as it used to do. Harrie, you did understand me more nearly than anybody else ever did. I still hope that some day we shall find One who really understands....

Let me tell you about the pictures you make for me when you try to see the places we have loved together. You know you quite often think of the manuka at Rotorua.... Yes, the tall bushes all powdered with little white starry blossoms and you and I walking along the narrow path, the bushes above our heads, and stopping to look at all our own special little springs of hot water—the clear blue one and the one that had the oil bubbling up and making scrolls and figures such as the Maoris used to make, and all the others.

Why, Harrie, are you crying?

You want to go on to our funny miniature mud volcano that we used to watch so many times—all those little plop-plops! Yes, and the big cone that we used to throw matches into and poke with sticks to see if we could make it erupt, and sometimes it did, a little....

Harrie, you know after I have written to you like this I feel so clean and pure...and then I go higher than ever and see such beautiful things. What a lot of writing you do...and I know it has done some good. How could all your pure desire to help be wasted?

[On the following communication, received a few days later, I find this notation in my own handwriting. "I came to my desk straight from reading Lodge's *Survival of Man,* in particular the part dealing with communications from Mr. Myers. The writing from the first was very strong, clear and rapid and accompanied by a sense of much excitement."]

Harrie, can you write now? You will please let me write without interruption. I want to tell you some of the things I have been thinking. I begin to think there have been others trying to write through you. Sometimes there seem to have been voices besides mine. Of course I can't be sure, but it seems possible. You have been reading some of those very things...You see I do know what you read when it is anything I am interested in, and I know every word you read in that book. . . .

Even Mr. Myers did not know what he was doing any more than I do—and Harrie, yes, he said he had to grope in fog and darkness when he was communicating, the same as I do, and I am where I can communicate all the time, so why should I be any better off than he was?

(You think that good news?)

Good news—yes! I am not so much worse off than others, after all! Yes, I am better off, for I am with you all the time and I can write to you hours every day and we can be as happy as we please! Harrie, I am so excited I make you write too fast . . .

You know I wanted you to read that book. I felt it had something in it for me. You smile, but I do know a thing or two sometimes. . . . I have known strange things, but also I have imagined even more about some things. You stop thinking, please. Why, so she did! Sometimes you really are obedient! . . . This is the very best news I have had for a long time, that Myers had as bad a time as I am having.

(He had been over only a month, you know, when that was written.)

No matter, he was communicating in fog and darkness just as I am. You think that I could go on up if I wanted to, but you know I don't want to. I want to stay with you. You did want me to stay—didn't you?

(I don't want to keep you in darkness.)

No, you would never have kept me from the light. Perhaps I couldn't go on, anyway, but what does it matter, Harrie, so long as we are together? . . .

What nonsense that is about the consciousness being in the hand. Of course the consciousness uses the hand—we'd better not go too fast. Never can tell, in this business. ... You think your hand, yes, and arm often—is controlled strongly by some will other than your own.... and you are made to write either detached words or words allruntogether likethis or

words	column
down	like
the	this
sheet	yes, of course you can do
in	otherwise if you will, it is
a	your hand, but there

is a power that pulls it to do something that is out of the usual way of writing.

(Yes, and that power comes in some way from you.)

Of course. Don't I know that?

(But they know nothing as to how it is done, and neither do we.)

Well, there is more truth than poetry in that.

(Haven't we written enough of this nonsense?)

You call this nonsense, do you? I call it pretty good common sense for a man in fog and darkness. ...

(F., do you seem to be specially conscious of my hand and what it does?)

Harrie, yes, I do. Not all the time, but a good deal of the time. I know whenever you even touch a piece of paper.

(Yes, I sometimes hear what you say at such times.)

Yes, you have heard me a good many times. It always gives me a thrill of excitement and I often say—Harrie is going to write now—and then if you don't write I am disappointed.

(You are more conscious of my hand than of anything else about me, in a physical sense?)

Yes, I am, because I always think of that little hand that does all the writing, and of course I am more conscious of that than anything else.

You are patient with me, Harrie, for you do think that perhaps some day we shall be able to know more than we do now and you think that if ever anyone can know anything about this business [of communicating] we ought to, for we are in such perfect relationship of love and confidence.... You know I want to help you and you know I have got intelligence, when I am able to use it, and we both believe that I am growing more able to use it.

It is something like being born over again and having to learn to use one's faculties or powers—or whatever they are in this state that I am in now . . .

You do take so long to go from one sheet to another. Can't help it, you say. No, I know you do the best you can.

Nothing whatever helps me so much as the knowledge of your love. I mean the real, spiritual love, and that is the greater part of your love for me. Yes, and of mine for you. You know that I love you in every way, but we both understand that the lower part of the earth-love must drop away as we go into the higher levels of this other life, and what is left is just the pure spiritual love.

What is this new feeling that I have for you?

Is it that I am nearer to you or farther from you?
Which? You no longer seem to be part of me as you did
before. O Harrie, don't let me go away from you, will
you? ...

There seems to be change in myself, and you are writing
as easily and rapidly as possible ... but that is not the
important thing. The important thing is that I want to tell
you what is the difference I feel, and it seems to me to be
this; that instead of feeling heavy and in thick fog I feel
buoyant and I am in the light. ...

Harrie, it is lovely! I feel clean and happy. You will
help me to write, won't you? You wish I could talk more
freely and not keep you so in the dark. Why, yes, you are
the one who seems in the dark now. ...

I tell you we are as nearly one as two beings can be and
retain any separate personalities. Think how close we were
at the last. You do know that that counts for something,
don't you? ... I have kept just so close to you in my thought
ever since. I don't even imagine that I could go on away
from you. ... I often wonder what is on beyond but I never
think that I want to go on if it would mean going away
from you or where I could not communicate with you.

You will try not to ask questions, won't you? You are
naturally full of questions, but no matter what you think
about it the fact is they do confuse me, so try not to, dear.
Just let me keep on as I am doing and I will try to tell you
all I can. ...

It gets you excited, doesn't it? You have so wanted me
to find the light. You think the better things will come.
Why yes, Harrie. This is better, and so why not more and
still more to come? Let me keep on writing, if you will,
please.

O my love! Why can't you share this with me? Better than earth? you wonder. Why, yes, dear. It is better than earth for I feel so light, as if I could just go floating off anywhere I chose—and perhaps I could, you think. No —not that. Don't tell me to go, for I want you with me when I do that....

Of all the experiences I have had yet this is the most encouraging, for I have never been in the light so long before.... Now don't get impatient, but you do, so what is the use of saying that. I do know what I am about.

You do interrupt me so. Well, what of it, that is what makes conversation, says you.... You do make me want to see you so, Harrie, when you talk like that! ...

How wonderful the whole every-day world of thought is!

I don't know whether I really see the things or whether I just imagine I see them, but they are real to me at the time . . . . but Harrie, I do feel your every emotion and know your every thought when you are writing and it does give me exquisite pleasure when you are thinking happy thoughts.

Now there is one thing—about time. Of course I know all about time so long as I am with you, for I know what you think. Every day you say—this morning—or—this afternoon—or—tonight—and so of course I know probably every day as it passes. But when I am not writing I have no more conception of time than if I had never known what it was.... You think of the time before we began to write. Nearly a year, you say, or quite a year before there was any clear communication.—There is as yet no clear knowledge of that time.

You are not writing well. Why are you so tired?

(I don't know.)

You are not very logical, are you? You expect me to know everything about myself, inside and out—yes, if there is any difference, which I suppose there is not, now—and you can't tell me such a simple thing as why you are tired. You say you don't know, and even I would know enough to answer that question, if you should ask me.

(Are you tired?)

No, not now, but when I am I know the reason why. It is usually because I have been trying so hard to tell you something when you would not let me, or trying to have you write when you couldn't....

Harrie, you are really very weak. Walked too much? Yes, perhaps that is it, but O Harrie, not so much—was it?

(No, but I am not much good at it now.)

Not like the time when you used to walk fourteen miles in New Zealand, is it? Yes, I have been remembering the places we loved.... You remember how we used to go fishing from ——— Island in the motor launch? And how I shot the gannet? ... Harrie, you do remember the gannet, don't you?

(Yes, it was a long shot.)

Why Harrie! Don't feel so badly ... MY OWN DEAR HARRIE! Yes, print it! Do anything to make it plain! ... Keep on writing.... Never mind about anything. Harrie! What would become of me if you got so you could not write? Don't you suppose it means more to me than it does to you, you poor little lonely woman? ...

I pause here in the course of the communications to give a few words of my own which were written just previous to the message next recorded. They have reference to a very strong and splendid realization which had come to me of a Mighty Presence—one whom I called The Master. He had appeared to me as the very Ideal of Manhood, greater and nobler than anything I had ever known or dreamed and more Real even than my own Beloved. In these words I tried to give some faint idea of the lasting impression which had been made on me.

"Yes, I like to think of the one I call The Master—my ideal for humanity; greater than any man we have yet known; supremely wise, kind, good; utterly true; of infinite patience; understanding all things; not beyond the touch of laughter; and with power that to the common mind of man might seem almighty, yet power capable of diminution or loss if it should be used selfishly or unworthily.

If you ask, can I conceive such a man living on earth now? I answer no; not in the fulness of his being. I see him too great for any one human body, as the bodies of men are today; too great for any one physical brain. And yet he is one and only one in his own realm of being.

What good for any common man to think of such a remote ideal? Because no one could even dream of such an ideal without approaching a step nearer to it. The very hope of the world lies in the cherishing of such dreams. The most powerful motive or spring of action that can make men better is in the vision of such ideal greatness and goodness.

Whether the attainment of such greatness would mean glory or sacrifice—who knows? and what matter?

I only know that the Being I see is one who speaks to the intellect as well as to the heart; he is able to inspire men not only to feel and to act, but to think and to understand.

My words are all inadequate, but there is not a man on earth today who would not desire to be like him if he could see him as I do."

It was after I had written the above and while my mind was still full of these thoughts that I received the signal to take up my pencil and the following message came.

O Harrie, will you let me write now?

(Wait a minute, please.) [This request was often necessary to enable me to get my paper, pencils, etc., in readiness for a long message.]

You always say—wait a minute—but Harrie, I have no idea how long a minute is.

(Well, my minutes are very variable, so that doesn't matter much.)

Yes, a woman's minutes are supposed to be variable, aren't they? You will please let me talk now. All that greatness sets me thinking. . . . I don't think I am that sort of person at all, for I shall always love power—I mean worldly power. . . . What is the use of being great if there is to be no result to the world of that greatness? . . . I know you think of a time when men can be influenced in ways that are not possible now, such as by thought direct, as I am influencing you.—Why Harrie, what came over you?

(Just the realization of what you are doing.)

I have never known you to feel that so strongly.—Well, you do understand what I mean and it is what you had in mind, isn't it? Then my way would naturally come first for it will be some time before this method of influencing human minds becomes common enough to be a means of using power on a large scale.

(Yes, but when it does come it makes a great man independent of all worldly considerations.)

Yes, truly. No votes needed, no popularity,—no anything but just power. Yes, of course, the moral qualities to use it greatly. You think what it might mean without moral qualities. Well, all kinds of men have power now, both good and bad, and when such means as this becomes general I suppose all kinds of men will use it too, so that there will be just the same sort of conflict there is now—always on a greater and more terrible scale, you think.

Well, war has grown greater and more terrible with the supposed progress of the world, hasn't it? Not a very encouraging prospect, you think.

No, but that is what men are making for themselves.

So much the more need, you think, for your kind of greatness. You mean the true wisdom and goodness—and you add that the truly wise man will be good.

Yes, Harrie, there is no doubt of that. Even for his own sake the really wise man will be good, for when men remember from one life to the next they will know what they have suffered because of their sin and their folly and then perhaps they will be better when they have the chance to begin over again on earth.

No, I am not talking Theosophy. I am talking just plain common-sense, taking reincarnation for granted as I must if I am to believe there is any sense at all in this suffering.

You think I speak as one who knows. Well, yes, you know I do, for I have told you that I suffered and I do still suffer.... You don't want me to talk about that now, do you?

I have made you write so very fast. Never mind, you got it. It is good to be able to say what I want to....

As you know, I am not one of those who know all about what is going to happen next or just what is going on all over the astral plane even now. My knowledge at present is limited to my own case and I have all I want to think about right in myself, and that is why I say a wise man will pattern his life differently to what I did mine if he wants to get along faster and better than I am doing....

There is a sort of astral perception, as I have told you, that is very all-embracing. Yes, astral consciousness, I called it. I say astral because that is a word that answers as well as any other. It doesn't signify what the word; it is the state that such a man finds himself in after death and that is all I mean.

You do want to know my thoughts, don't you?

Why do you think my thoughts are more valuable now than when I was on earth?

You think you always did like to know my thoughts.

Yes, I know you did—and now you think I have a new point of view.

Well, yes, in a way I have, but still not so very new after all. It is rather that I have nothing to do but think. On earth there are so many other things a man can do that he can get out of thinking if he wants to, but here where there is nothing to distract, one must think. ·

You believe that is the purpose of this period, in part at least, for those who are capable of thinking. Yes, I believe that...and in my own case it seems to be the only thing I have to do....

You begin to hear me, don't you? ... It seems as if I must be nearer to you when I am writing than at other times. You won't think that I am far away at any time, will you? for perhaps that does send me away. No, I don't want to go away. I will wait for my knowledge of other things till we can go together....

When you come to write, why not meditate first, trying to fix your thought on me, not as I am, but on that ideal you have and which you want me to become? for it does make a difference, and so why not give me the benefit of that high thinking more than you do? ... Help me to the best thought and feeling and the highest purpose you can.

You know I have not been like this long, for it does seem as if I had just been living in my imagination and not the highest part of it, either.... You don't need to think there is any danger of my falling back into that old state again, for there has been a steady progression upward all the time from the very first consciousness I had....

Now I shall begin to think and know myself and while no doubt I shall suffer more, it will really be a purgative suffering and I will endure it gladly ....for if desire and purpose can change a man I shall be a new man indeed when I come back to earth again, and I do believe that I shall do that. What sense in it all, otherwise?

You feel just full of thanksgiving. Yes, let the old things drop behind. Coming into the clearer mental vision, you say. Yes, that is undoubtedly what this period is for—to learn to know myself truly, as I am, before I can allow myself to see or know others.

You did not like to write that 'allow myself,' but Harrie it is true, for I do know that there are other beings all around me and that if I wanted to I could see them—perhaps—talk with them I know; but I don't want to till I am sure of myself—of my truth, my purity, and my strength. . .

You think there must be help from higher planes whether I am conscious of it or not. Well, let us hope so. . . . We don't know anything yet, Harrie dear, but I do know that you help me. And you darling, you must think that when I am a little stronger I shall be able to help you. Pray God I may be.

. . . When you begin to think of man you ought to know that you have got a new element of being to reckon with and that is the reasoning power. That is one thing you never seem to take into account. . . . It is the greatest new factor that has been brought into action since the beginning of life.—You might just keep on writing instead of stopping after every word, if you don't mind.

This power of reasoning is such a great thing that it would inevitably result in a new order of evolution. I mean it would naturally set up new processes altogether different from anything previously in operation. . . . You can hardly over-estimate the change that would result when a being is developed self-conscious to the degree that he can intelligently help or hinder his own evolution.

Don't treat that idea as if it were of small account. It is of more account than all the rest of your thoughts put together so far as understanding the destiny of man is concerned. And by destiny I mean what we commonly think of as his "future," whether in other lives to come on earth or in some far-away planet or realm of space unknown to you at present.

Harrie ... you have stopped everything that helped to develop or expand your consciousness and you are shutting yourself in such a narrow place that I am not able to get through. Will you begin to think of what you are doing? Meditate,—I have asked you to ... You must be willing to help me. You must get back to your meditation—yes, and your faith....

Write as often as you can and think of me as much as you can and love me always, greatly and simply and just all the ways we ever have loved—all the ways, for we have been true lovers.

You do give me light.... I wait to see the light and then I say, 'Harrie is loving me!'

... You think the pencil wants to scrawl instead of writing. Yes, perhaps it does, a sort of careless, impatient feeling—too much trouble to write properly. Yes, I know I sometimes do feel that way. Getting tired of communicating, you think.

No, Harrie, not that but—getting tired of not being able to say what I want to. And whose fault is that?

Well, whose? ...

This is F—and I am trying to talk to you just as I would if I were in the flesh; I am not trying to compose a literary essay.

Harrie, we are not going back, we are going forward and things will be different. It is no use to think we can go back to something that we were two or three months ago; we shall not do that and it is no use trying for we are not moving in that direction.

I tell you that I know more now than I ever have before and I want to tell you many things if you will let me. There is no need to flourish so much, that is an unnecessary strain to put on you, but you can control that if you will— only don't stop writing. Hold your hand firmly and don't let it dance around so after every word....

I did cultivate a style of utmost simplicity because it seemed easier for you to take short words and simple sentences, but now I no longer want to do that ; I want to write in my own natural style.

There is change in me.... You know I have wanted to tell you about those old times when we first thought we had found the Master ... there is still a great deal of confusion with me but I do believe that we came into contact or relationship with a very great spiritual Being ... One whose presence filled us both with love and reverence and under whose influence we were lifted to regions higher than we have ever known since....

Many great truths were given us.... Harrie, you do believe in him still, and so do I, and that thought fills you with content—your old word.

Reality! Such peace.

.... You know, after all, just being in this high region is the greatest good we can ask. It is better than anything

I can write for we both know once more that the highest
is true.

Harrie, Christ is the highest truth there is for man. You
see I have found him again, after all this time.

You for Truth, I for Love, just as before . . . .

Don't begin to doubt. I tell you that is the worst down-
ward-pulling force I know. Faith lifts us above, pulls
us up.

(F., you say I am all for Truth and you for Love, but
you were not a lover of mankind in general when you
were on earth. You had even less patience than I with
the dull, ugly ruck of humanity.)

. . . . All the same I know that Love is the one thing
that redeems such folks. You know what I mean . . . . the
love that is shed on them from the Christ, who did give his
life for their sake.

If they can realize that he did so love them, it stirs a
spark of love in them—a higher sort of love than they have
known—and that is the thing that redeems,—belief in one
who loves you in spite of all the wrong you have done. It
may not do it for all natures, but what else is there for
a man or a woman who has been really sinful and weak?
What else?

(Yes, that is the hope of the sinful. But I was thinking
not so much of sinners as of the merely common-place.)

Harrie, they are the most hopeless ones. Without imagination, neither good nor bad, just muddle-headed—yes, and
comfortable, so they don't feel the need of any great
change—just a little more comfort or pleasure is all they
want. I suppose they are a large proportion. No, not the

bulk. The bulk are the poor, ignorant, vicious, weak, down-trodden ones and they do need Christ.

We do lift each other, don't we? Sometimes one has faith and sometimes the other, but you are going to try and keep your faith this time....

Harrie, when I see, I no longer have faith, I have knowledge....

You ought not to be so up and down now...perhaps we can be more stable.

(These alternations of light and dark, of high and low, seem from what I read to be the experience of all who try to attain to knowledge of the higher realms.)

Yes, perhaps, but if we fully understand it we need not be so troubled. We can understand that it is meant to enlarge our comprehension and perhaps also to enlarge our sympathies.... You still love, and you do want to help, and you still want truth. One never knows how much can be borne, Harrie, till the test is made, so you ought to be glad you have learned your weakness.

Now you can begin to strengthen yourself and the very first thing to do is to come back to the point where you were when you first found me, and that is to believe in the power of love and of Christ's love for us, and the pure desire to help the sinful and unfortunate....

You must not think that all I need is once or twice to be helped. I need a great deal of help and shall need it, probably, for a long time to come.... You feel so overwhelmed at the thought, but that is not the way to feel. Of course it means dropping down, but we have found that we can mount up....

You shall not ask one question, Harrie, please. No, you can't help in that way.

You are so very patient, poor Harrie ... all you need is to know that I want you and you leave everything and come to me. You do wish I could tell you more about these changes in myself, but then you always go off when I talk about not knowing things. That is one truth that you can't seem to accept. .... You are so very rebellious, but what is the use?

I am in the condition that has been brought about by my past life and whatever you may think about it, I know it is just what I have made and·that I have got to endure it till I am—[writing confused].

Harrie, yes, love is all I need .. You are divine love to me.

(F., you know we have received help from some higher Power when we have asked for it. You have felt it as well as I.) ·

You know I did, so many times, like the very breath of the great Spirit. Truth, yes, and Wisdom. . . . I never called on him without feeling the response; the highest, greatest and best of all that I can conceive—that is what comes when I call on him.

Yes, Christ always, to me, but your ideal too—different, not so tender nor so compassionate but full of understanding. ... Christ—the Master—I can't separate them the way you do. You always think of the personalities, but I think of the great, wide, universal aspect; all the world can share in it; love, truth, peace, good will.

Think what those words mean—good will. Not as we usually say them but in the sense you use the word will—

the will itself being good and good only and all the time. That would be redemption, perfection.

Of course every man needs redemption. Men are not so perfect but that they sin sometimes—do the thing they know to be wrong—and when they do that they need to be redeemed. Yes, to have the will purified, that is just it, so they will desire always to do what they know to be right.

(F., do you think men always know what is right?)

Harrie, yes, they do. They know but they don't want to know and they won't believe their own knowledge, or won't admit it. They do deny it to themselves but they know. I believe no man lives who does not know when he does wrong.

You question that. No, one man does not know all right and all wrong but he knows his own right and wrong. That is what I mean. He knows what is wrong for him. He is not asked to judge for another; not on the spirit plane at least. We men on earth ask one man to judge for many others in some instances, but here each man is his own judge, or so it is with me and I am sure it must be so with all.

How else could it be and be true justice?

You understand what I mean. I know exactly wherein and how far I fall short of what I knew. I—my Real Self as you call me on this plane . . . . I know where and how I turned away from the very highest I knew and went down into the depths deliberately after what I conceived to be pleasure . . . . and I knew that every time I did that I vitiated something in me that was pure and high—but I did it!

Who could tell me more than I know about all that?

.... You begin to rise to the thought of the cleansing that comes through this self-knowledge. O but it is a terrible thing to go through! ....

That is the thing I live for, Harrie .... when I can feel that I need never think of it again. Yes, that will come. It will drop from me as the physical body has gone and will be thought of no more than I think of that.

(F., I am always trying to get a clearer idea of your present condition.)

How can I tell you? This is so different. You don't seem to understand that I do try to tell you, but if you doubt, I can't. ...

My personality is not the thing that matters. The thing that matters is that you know I LIVE AND LOVE YOU. You don't want that old personality, do you? You want the Greater Self, don't you? Will you please try to forget this old personality?

(But often when I come to write it seems to be that lower personality who speaks. Do you mean that I should not answer at such times?)

Of course answer, but turn it into a demand on the higher, for that is the way you help the lower. Demand the higher by turning all your thoughts, as you write, to him.

I know that you have a true desire to help those whom you love to belief in spiritual things and you want knowledge more that you may convince others than because you need it yourself. For you know, in spite of your backslidings, that the spirit does live only you fear that it may have a more difficult and painful task than you like to think of.

You are really trying to walk the razor edge, aren't you? You think it is easier now you understand that the destiny of others as well as yourself hangs on how you succeed. Yet you must know that this is true of every act in life, whether before or after the change that you call death.

I do begin to know that I am free of some of the things that held me to earth and I can now look up and see what heights lie above me. The one thing I want before I try my wings is just YOU! You to be with me, as I am, not you there in your plain black dress as I see you now, writing alone at your desk.

Yes, always alone. Not alone in spirit but always alone in the body. So much it does not do to think about....

Harrie, what a wise creature you are to think so little about the past. Good or bad, it lies behind us and if we have learned its lessons there is nothing more it can do for us or we for it, so let it fade as fast as it will.

You want to keep the beauty and the love. Why yes, they are of the spirit. You can't lose them!

My own dear love, won't you try to be a little more patient with me? I am not infallible but I am trying to rise to that region where there is truth, but I have to grope my way in what is spiritual darkness, even though I no longer feel myself in that total blackness of vision that I did at first. You will help me? . . .

You must help me by keeping to the faith that there is One who Knows and One who Can and Will Help. . . .

O my God! Make me worthy to help her to believe that I am her true lover F. and let us go hand in hand all the way, through darkness or through light!

'O my Beloved!' You go around singing that half the time. You do feel happier about me; is that it, love, my Harrie? . . . .

You lift me so high . . . endless vistas, illimitable, un-fathomable! . . .

Harmony of light, color, sound—

Love is harmony.

Harrie, you are just full of love and remembrance, aren't you? You do love to think of our true companion-ship. . . . Yes, there is peace all through me. How lovely it is to be at peace again!

You know I am happy because I do know there is power we can draw on—not just our own. You know how you like to feel that I can help you? Well, I have you, of course, but I do want to feel that there is power high above me—not too greatly above—and the Master does seem to feel that need, and when Dr. S told you. . . . . I thought, now perhaps I can find help even if I have lived a useless life, for here I am getting clear of all that old nature and wanting to become better and willing to serve if I can find One who is Good and who will help me to be more unselfish.

Then when those great words came to us I did believe they came from him, and then came the power and that splendid light and sense of goodness, and yes, there was both peace and an urgent need of some kind of outlet for the power I felt stirring in me. . . .

We will not think we can often be so honored as to hear his very words, but let us turn to what we believe to be our own proper work and use for it this power that springs up in us.

The communication that follows is one of the most remarkable in this book.

The writing at first was trivial in character but the control of my hand was very strong, increasingly so, and after F.'s cry of "O why?" there came a sudden sense of soaring and the pencil wrote in large, fair letters with a lightness of touch that is indescribable. I had never dreamed that pencil could touch paper so softly and smoothly.

It seemed to me that I scarcely breathed, even when my thoughts responded to the words that were being written, my whole being was so flooded with the sense of awe and mounting rapture.

Harrie, you are full of good thoughts now. You can see that I am happy and I feel very intelligent.—You know that is a joke. Two reasons for using that word—one, to make you laugh; the other because it is a favorite word of yours and I am getting to like it myself. It is a useful word. . . .

You need not talk, I know all about you. Yes, let me talk for you do not know all about me. . . .

And now let me tell you something you have long wanted to know. This is a wordless realm that I am in. Wherever this is, I do not think in words or communicate in words, I am sure of that. . . . I give you my thought direct and the words are all your own and the reason for their simplicity and directness is that the thought is of an order that must find such expression in your mind. I cannot say how it might be expressed if it were sent through a different mentality than yours. . . .

Harrie, I want so to see! O why, do you suppose?

(Have you ever asked if you might know the reason why you see so little?)

Yes I have, again and again, and the only answer I ever get is—Wait. Wait. . . .

You think I have been taught?

You know I am sort of dazed. I seem to be going higher and higher all the time.

Where am I?

O this is wonderful! You ought to see the colors—all full of light, like rainbows, only more colors and so very luminous!

Where are you, Harrie?

You can still write, but this is Heaven!

Here are the angels all in white. Here is heavenly music. Here is the very Throne of God. There is the River of Life. Yes, a great river, crystal clear, and all so pure and lovely.

No more tears.

Where is Harrie?

She will come when you are all clean and white like those you see here.

Harrie, can you see me here?

(No, my love, I cannot see you. I can only write.)

You are still writing. You know why I think of you so all the time—because you are my only star of love and if I lost you I should be in the dark without a light to guide me.

You think the thought of the Master had such power, to give me that fair vision.

No, it is not a vision, it is all real, only I may not stay here long.

Who can say how long I may stay when there is love on earth that can sit so still and write so that I may share this beauty and light with her?

> You are my love, my life, my light,
> You are the one to whom I turn.
> O must I go from this to night
> And ever more my way re-learn
> To these far heights so steep and white?
>
> Let me abide, O Lord of Life,
> Let me abide. This is my right!
> I am Thy Child! I am Thy Son!
> The Christ has given his life for me.
> Thou art—

My own, my dear, my love, my all! Keep me—

NO. NO. NOT YET.

You are so still you scarcely breathe.

I don't know whether you hear me.

You hear me—and what am I saying? What am I singing? Great music. Music of the spheres—so wonderfully sweet. Harmony piled on harmony. . . .

Why wait so long, my love? [A pause.]

(Where are you, F?)

Why Harrie, I am right here with you, and you are so still, so quiet, so calm. Yes, Peace.

You sent me up when you told me that the Master had taught me, Himself. . . . Realms of pure love and life. . . .

You are so strong for my sake.

Master, so be near us ever. Guide and direct us always, Great Master of us both. . . .

[A little later these words came.]

He bids you give this message to the world.

Never shall such true love go unrewarded so far as his power extends in any realm of all the worlds while there is human personality to love and be loved.

This communication is, to me, too miraculous for any attempt at explanation. Whatever the real nature of the experience so far as F. was concerned, to me it was a Revelation—the more so for being so far from any belief I had held in such a Heaven of whiteness and glory. I saw nothing, but bare words cannot tell what I was made to feel. I can only say that I know, now, what worship and adoration can be.

Even in this great moment the hampering consciousness of the lower self did not wholly leave me. It is not easy to express that sense of double consciousness. I felt the mighty rhythm of unheard music around and through me, yet as soon as I became aware that the pencil was writing verse I doubted the adequacy of that earth-instrument and so halted and broke and partially lost the words which were striving to shape themselves.

Some time later my thoughts had reverted to this vision and I was trying to frame, for myself, some idea of its reality which I could reconcile with my

ability to write while it was in progress, when the
signal came to take up my pencil and the following
"conversation" ensued.

Harrie, you do believe that I saw that, don't you?

(Yes, I believe that you saw it, but I can hardly believe
that while I wrote you were transported to the Very Heaven,
so perhaps it was a sort of reflection within yourself.)

What is the difference?

(I do not know that there is any difference. I do not
know but you can truly be in the highest heaven there is
and be right here with me all the time.)

Harrie dear, you know the highest truth there is in the
universe when you know that.

More than a year after the above was written I
read for the first time Swedenborg's *Heaven and Its
Wonders and Hell* (originally published in 1758). I
had, strangely enough, managed to go through all my
life up to this time with no knowledge, direct or indi-
rect, of his visions and writings. I found in this book
confirmation of many of my own experiences and par-
ticularly of this glimpse into Heaven.

Swedenborg says:

"When certain spirits wished to know what heavenly
joy is they were allowed to feel it to such a degree
that they could no longer bear it . . . for before their
interiors are opened spirits can be taken up into heaven
and be taught about the happiness of those there. I
saw them in this quiescent state for about half an hour,

and afterwards they relapsed into their exteriors. . . . They said that they had been among the angels in heaven and had there seen and perceived amazing things . . . . that could not be described in human language or fall into ideas which partake of anything material. . . . Thus are they permitted to learn what true spiritual and heavenly good is."

I resume now my extracts from the communications as they came, in the days following this heavenly vision.

You can be very happy when you once think of the whole time that we have been writing and of the change you know has come in me and in what is around me.

Harrie, that was all a test of what we could do, and no single experience is vain or wasted and you may feel perfectly sure that I am in a far higher state than I was, even if I do not express myself so well just now.

I feel another being, higher, finer, purer, nobler,—with great aspirations and full of faith and belief in all that is good and such a sense of exaltation! Light—yes, all radiant light! No darkness ever now unless I go away down and that does not often happen. . . .

You just floated all around me then, Harrie, like a little white spirit looking to see what you could see, and finally you said, 'O, here you are!' and settled right down by my side and here you are still, smiling. . . . I only feel you here with me or in me—one with me—sweet, serene, peaceful and loving me, and that is enough for one man, or ought to be, till he does really find his own Master. . . .

Harrie, love, I am sure he said:

Tell her she shall come to me with him as she desires and when that time comes there shall be no failure to understand and no shadow of doubt in all her being.

Listen to this. He says:

F. is still fighting for his soul and it is and will be a long, · hard fight. . . . It is true that he can never remain permanently on the upper planes or be all that you long to have him be until he perfectly attains the victory over the lower nature, but do not be too sure that you can help him by too great insistence on immediate conquest.

Let him go on as he has done, alternating his battles with glimpses of the worlds he will some day attain in his full strength.

You do love him and that is the greatest help he can ever have from the earth plane and I do help him from my own realm of truth and strength and peace.

I give here a few words that came on one of the days when there seemed to be a confusion of voices and other personalities coming between F. and myself. At the end came this tribute which was too spontaneous and delightful to be omitted from my record.

She is the bulliest writer we've ever known—steady as a tree. . . . Don't you see why? A tree is one thing that can bend to the winds of Heaven but has its roots deep in Earth.

You are so calm . . . for you know that there is Unity back of it all, don't you? and that you are steadily reaching up to the One and so you need not be troubled by the appearance of confusion.

You see Your Own Self knows; so you can rest quiet and
wait for that better knowledge to come down to you, as it
will. No, not only in sleep; at any and all times when you
are quiet and give it a chance.

It must come—we can't go on forever just we two in a
universe all to ourselves, and that is just what we made for
ourselves;—yes, and what we wanted, but we can't end like
this, can we? . . . .

You must be strong to know that you can still love me
most and yet love others and extend your love and help
to all who will come. We are selfish, that is our greatest
fault you know, and it is so futile. . . . You will find that
you cannot lose me by loving and helping others. I shall
always be near you and we shall go hand in hand . . . growing more, not less, in every good way.

The soul of a man and the soul of a woman truly mated
can never be separated. They are one in all the realms of
the universe.

Only a good man can comprehend love.

When a man is as fully conscious of the mental and
spiritual qualities that are attractive in a woman as he is
now conscious of her physical attractions, marriage will be
on a new basis.

You want to feel that I must be willing to learn all there
is to learn at once. What you would learn, you think that
I must learn, and that is not possible. I am not you and
I cannot take from any experience what you would take;
so you must not think that I am through with pain or the

necessity of it just because you would have learned its lesson in a given time while I am still in the midst of suffering and likely to be for some time to come.

I know I need to suffer! Yes, I want to suffer till I am wiser. That is the thing I have asked for. . . . I must do the work now that I failed to do then; for I am resolved that when I come back to earth again I will know what is worth doing and worth being and so I must in some way get the knowledge here that I failed to get when I had the chance on earth. . . . There is enough good in me to make it worth while to make a special effort to eliminate all that is worst and that would interfere with any real usefulness in another life.

So you see I do know something of what I am undergoing, yes, and why. And yet I do not always have this knowledge and often when you come to write you find me in the throes of some agony of doubt or worse and I am not able to talk about other things and I am in too much pain at the moment to know why I am suffering. So that is why I wanted to tell you. . . .

You can help me only by knowing beyond a faintest shadow of doubt that all is for my good and that I shall bear what I have to willingly, and that I do know when you give me love and it is a healing thing to me.

I was called one day to take the following message from a meditation in which I was comparing the activities of human life to a performance by a vast orchestra.

Let me show you the wonderful thing I see in the midst of these thoughts of yours, Harrie.

I see a palace; white, gleaming, curiously carved; all surrounded by color flashing in great circling waves. All the center of the picture is blinding light and all around is color, and—you see what I do!

Yes! There are Beings who weave that color into such beautiful harmonies. Music, you say! You saw those who compose the thoughts and those who carry the thoughts into expression. Harrie, so do I. But these are all emanations from the one great light! Yes, they come from that great palace so white! so blinding light!

No, I can't tell it. You don't see this part as I do, for to me all is the One who is the Center. He is color, not alone light. All is Himself. How can there be anything that is not Himself?

The Composer is not, as you think, one who creates a harmony. He simply carries out the will of the One who is All.

(But there *is* disharmony in life.)

Harrie, the elements that make the harmony are always there, it is only the men or the individuals who destroy the harmony because they will not listen or will not see the purpose that is eternal and is in all creatures if they will only listen or look to the center of their own being. All that you think is bad is just the elements that have not been drawn into the harmony. . . . Harmony is the law of being. There is no such thing as energy without some purpose and that purpose is pure harmony or perfection— or whatever better word for it you can find, for you do see what I mean!

O Harrie! Never think that man is greater than his Creator!

You will, please, let me tell you. I have said that I heard
the great Voice. Well, that voice does speak but I do not
repeat to you all that it says. I could not, for it is strong
and fills me with its reverberations and then I have to think
what was said and I do find words of my own for the
impression it has left with me.

Harrie, do not dismiss it so carelessly. I am trying to
put into words what cannot be told. . . . I do try to make
you understand—it is all so different. . . .

I am conscious in me of much that is new, strange, queer,
great,—oh! all sorts! But there is hardly one thing that
I can put into any form of expression that would mean
anything to you. . . .

Where is the miracle in the whole world equal to this
one little fact that you and I can be so close, so far apart;
so one, so different; so much to each other, so nothing that
one can see or touch? . . . a very mystical word I want to
use. Must you fail me so soon, O Harrie?

The Absolute you think so much and know so little about,
. . . . what is the Absolute but—not will, but Consciousness? and if that is so, why what are we but bits of the
total of consciousness? And only the united whole can
possibly be said to know itself or to know the whole about
anything.

You think then each separated part could know the whole
about itself; but even that is not so, for no part can know
very much about itself unless the whole organization is
taken into account. How can the part comprehend the
whole? And without knowing the whole what can the part
understand of its own peculiar office or function? .

Go back to your old conception of the cells of the body. What can a tissue cell know of itself? Only a minute fraction of the truth, for it can have no understanding of its relative importance in the structure of the body or of the interdependence of the parts which it helps to constitute; and without this knowledge what does the knowledge of its own infinitesimal self amount to? Nothing at all. . . .

True, the physical brain is the organ of consciousness in the body, but consciousness is not confined . . . [to it] and how do you know whether it is really dependent on the brain even for what we commonly suppose? It may have other means of acquiring information even about physical matters.

I seem to be able to know several things about you. . . .

Harrie . . . . these are the words I hear in myself:

Poor, imperfect, struggling soul, you do indeed aspire too high but you aspire truly. You shall some day reach all that now seems so distant, though the way may be long.

Be patient. Never fear. Never doubt. There is One who knows all the suffering and all the temptation and all the sin and the ceaseless struggle.

Be brave. Take peace, and thank God for the love that has been sent to go with you all the way.

> The next communication came on a day when I had been reading Helen Keller's *World I Live In*. I read for two or three hours, absorbed in the book, and on laying it down was surprised to receive an imperative signal to take up the pencil. The writing that came was firm, clear, and very rapid; the sense of it wholly surprising to me.

Harrie—let me tell you where I have been. You come with me—try.

This is a little blind girl in the slums of the city. She lives in a queer little tumble-down house near one of the great thoroughfares.

The man you see with her . . . is not always kind to her, although he is not cruel. He is so busy he does not think what it must be like to be blind and so he will not take the trouble to point out the wonder and beauty of God's universe to the little blind girl who sits near him so patiently all day long.

You ask if he is a cobbler. You thought of that because I said he sits all day. No, he is not a cobbler. He sits at his task of sorting old rags and that is what keeps him so busy; for it requires constant vigilance lest something of possible value should escape him and be thrown into the heap that represents, even to a rag-picker, refuse.

Yes, this is a story with a moral. Let the little blind girl represent you as you sit there, pencil in hand, waiting so patiently. You are blind, but you know that there is a world of wonder up here, or so you think, that you would love to hear all about.

And then here am I, just picking over rags all the time—all the accumulated rubbish of my last earth-life; memories of every least thing I ever did, said, felt or thought; trivial things, unworthy, glad, sorry; all kinds, all mixed in together; most of them worn, tattered; little beauty and less utility here you would think if you could see them as I see.

But here is my material out of which I have to lay the foundation for my next earth life.

H.—do you wonder that I pore over my task so steadily that I quite forget my little blind girl waiting to be told of the glories of God's great spiritual universe which lies here somewhere? Just where I do not yet know myself because I am working in a little darkened hut and what lies outside I know scarecly more than you.

You heavenly love! The little blind girl slips a hand in mine and says, 'No matter, I love you.'

You think of all the precious fragments in among all the useless scraps which I pick over in my quest. Yes, there are some beautiful bits here.

Not one word of anything that has been written is more absolutely truthful than this little allegory.

Harrie, will you believe that I do vary so all the time? I can't tell you why, but this is the truth. . . This is the strange thing, that there are the things I want you to know but I simply cannot tell you so it can be written. It goes from me in some way that is not accessible to the one who writes . . . . I live in extremes. Very little middle ground. You understand.

This is what I do. Say here is a black, ugly thought. . . .

Now when this thought comes into shape I see it so false I am always tempted to hate it, but when I can remember, I say: You poor thought, so utterly false. Why, this is the truth! And as I say these words that thought changes, grows pure, rosy, melts.

Reality . . . lastingness . . . the Eternal Changeless One that is always there, whoever or whatever comes or goes.

We know it. . . . I tell you we know it, just for the very good reason that there is a spark of that same reality in ourselves, so you know yourself and I know myself—and

Harrie, my love, my mate, I do believe that you and I are closely linked all the long way we have come, for we are so sure of each other. Surely not many two souls are as sure of the reality of each other as we are. . . .

I have come now, in point of chronology, to December, 1919. From this time on there is increasing change in the nature of the communications. There is frequent allusion to new conditions ever more difficult to describe. At times there was complaint as to the difficulty of getting me to write. There was no more flourishing, no more hard bearing down and rapid wearing away of pencil leads. Often the touch was so light as to leave the writing almost indistinct and long pauses would fall between the end of one paragraph and the beginning of the next.

The Great Voice comes often, seeming to break through the thoughts which F. is trying to give me and at such times the touch grows firm and the words sweep out on the page in large, clear letters,—words of spiritual truth reflecting a light that was not seen by F. or by me while he was on earth.

You are like one who dimly sees the sun shining on remote hill-tops and hardly dares hope for it to reach his little valley, but the sun rises over the highest mountain tops and shines into the lowliest valley and you and I are sure to feel its rays on us before long. So Harrie, love, let us wait in confidence.

Harrie—still loving life!

You are altogether right. Life should be loved. It is made to be loved. Yes, it can be made so utterly lovely if

men will only see the things that make it so and desire
them; so blind because we don't yet see our own possi-
bilities!

You see all that is good and beautiful so clearly only
through the spiritual sense that I have wakened in you. You
saw no more than others before we began to write.
[True! H.]

Harrie, the one who teaches is not one who tells us the
truth in the sense you mean. He only brings us into relation
with truth so that we may acquire it for ourselves, each in
his own way. . . . You want truth to be told you but it is
impossible to tell you what you are not ready to understand.

Keep the way open so the higher knowledge can enter.
It is in such effort—for true meditation is effort—that one
is led to contact the divine knowledge always waiting a
chance to come in.

Not one thought of yours that is not an invitation to
another thought to enter and abide. . . .

Your mind is open to all the thought in the universe that
you can take in and make your own.

You alone can commence the upward climb to us. Only
through some effort that brings you to this pitch of concentration is it possible for you to receive my words.

Try to keep the concentration. Use the one central
thought of your Master, then gather around this central
thought the characteristics you wish to acquire. Make it
your purpose to be strong, steadfast, equable, pure,
loving. . . .

Names live in the higher realms as truly as thoughts. All world-known names are words of power.

Consciousness is truly like the ocean. You draw mighty currents to yourself when you turn your thoughts to these great and powerful names. . . .

Never believe that you are deserted by Me. In every need call on Me. You may not always be conscious of the voice, but always the answer comes.

What need of thinking more of personality when spirit with spirit can meet? You see me now, but not so strongly the personality as you used to. Just now I seem to you to be lacking in form, which is just as I am. While you see only the past I seem shapeless, for so much of that past is gone. . . .

Every thought you make of a future self that is still I helps to build me into that greater form. All that is to be waits on us, for we are the builders, both of us, since we are true mates and can co-operate with each other as truly, yes, as definitely, as it is said we can co-operate with God, the unseen builder of the universe.

Harrie, all life is real. This is real to me—yes, very real. Not in a sense you can comprehend, but nevertheless it is real. Often very painful, but so was the earth life. . . .

Always from the first there was a struggle, typified in many strange experiences in you . . . I was always living in the midst of such experiences, not witnessing them. Every experience I pass through is just as real, living actuality to me at the time of its happening as anything in my life has ever been. . . .

You understand that, due to your constant writing and questioning, I have from the first tried, however feebly, to understand what was going on in myself in a way that would never have occurred to me if I had been left to myself. This, we do know, was all part of a purpose, not chance.

(F., I want to understand more about words—our words.)

. . . . You never will understand much till you learn to hold your thought to one point long enough to let the truth come to you. . . .

So long as we are not too etherealized—use it for want of a better word—we may dimly sense the earth-words and so try to put thoughts into forms that can be apprehended by those still connected with the instrument of physical consciousness—the brain. . . . When I go to a higher plane there is no longer any perception of earth words and I could not then even faintly know what words would be chosen by you as your record of what you perceive in me and so if you were quite wrong in the impression you received through all the many strata of consciousness that intervene, I should have no possible means of knowing; therefore such effort even is discouraged, because it generally leads to mistaken conceptions.

You see just a reflection of myself in you . . . . all through the reflection—and that word is not the exact truth, only just a faint groping for the truth—your love has so beautified it and purified that some beauty is living in every particle of it. . . .

You are the soul of love in me. I am the soul of love in you. That is union.

There is in me much that is dainty, fairy-like, fanciful, as you know. All that stirs within myself, wakes, grows active, seeks to mix in your consciousness. . . . All these thoughts are pleasant but not the less distracting for all that. We must not forget that we are on the way to something better.

It is true that when I go on as I am going now all those trifling thoughts go to sleep in me and I feel other thoughts waking, much greater . . . dim, yes, only vague forms, not clearly defined—that is why I can't express them.

These are such things as we need. By these thoughts we grow—expand to greatness! . . . . I, F., see here still, all in me, these great dim thoughts rousing as if from long, long sleep. I must have been on the way to greatness before. Yes, it must be so, for these are thoughts that have been in me for a long time, but dormant. Not much growth afforded them in the earth-life recently ended.

You see how strong I am, though you are not so easy to make see this; but try. All those little fanciful thoughts raise a protest when I come here . . . O Harrie, such grandeur is more than beauty! . . . . These are things we don't know how to express.

Yes, all is in me. Life flows into me from heights beyond. . . . Yes, there is something in you to mix with the greatest thoughts I can even conceive. . . .

O Love, what are the words to even hint at these things?

Here, above the regions where we have been, I no longer see any forms that annoy, harass, or irritate. All is serene, tranquil. Yes, strength is here—only, too high. . . .

I am F. —. —. and I am more than that. All that he aspired to be, meant to be, was and shall be, I am.

You see I do come back to all the Christian words of truth. Yes, for this is going to be the new era—just coming into a true knowledge of Christ . . . . and that is love; love for all the weak, unworthy, yes, even the wicked, the base; all that so effectually hides from man the wonderful truth that he is Son of God.

I am here where I feel great and noble thoughts flow into me as simply as breath flows into the body in the clear, pure mountain air. . . .

I often hear these great voices and when they speak I learn more than ever you dreamed. Some of it can be put in words, some must not be told to any one yet.

I am always asking, 'Who is this that speaks?'

Sometimes I am told; other times there is no answer.

Often I hear, 'Who are you?' I say 'F—. —. —.' Then the same voice will say, 'I am your present helper. You may ask me such questions as you see fit, but do not be distressed if all are not answered.'

Then we may talk till some one else comes along. . . .

Let me try to clear up this matter for you. . . .

You see, I am always just F. in one sense; but of course I am never alone in that if I think one least thought that leads to another being,—divine, human, or lower; in me is formed some sort of image of that being. . . . All in me is this reflection . . . and as I grow clearer I see these images in me and as they rise to my higher consciousness I then know whether any given image is correct or not. At such times I am in light; all pure, clear, transparent; and then I know. . . .

When your thought turns to the Master, he answers; but if I am then trying to talk to you myself I may even shut off his thought from reaching you. Only when we both go to him clear and transparent those great words come. . . . At our highest we are so one that we see a glory!

The Master,—Christ. They are not separated in me as you try to separate them. . . . It is this way. Whenever I think of one, that one is so full of his superior—the Master is full of Christ,—Christ, Son of God—all come to the one who turns his thought to even the lowest symbol of divinity that he can make live in him. . . .

Always they speak. Always the truth is there. All I can do is to let it pass through me to you. You think it is personal to you; that is not the way it is. It is there for all, like the sunlight. All I do is take it and pass it on to you. Your brain is what makes it seem personal to you. . . .

Help me to live in this clear light. Here there is truth. Here I can discriminate. What strange folly to live down below in such clouds and fog!

Redemption is purification of the will. . . . I will cleanse myself absolutely and when that is accomplished I dedicate myself to service in the name of Christ. Not church but Love, for Christ is Love.

You MUST let him speak in me, Harrie. Call him what you will, it is the Voice that speaks and his words fill me with holy peace.

Love comes into every human heart, it may be only once, it may be many times in a life.

Cherish it, nourish it, help it to grow, for it is the very breath of the Spirit of God in man and all else is given for its growth and evolution.

Life is given for this one purpose; to perfect God Himself by evolving love in every atom of His universe.

Harrie, you go back to remotest antiquity and look forward to ages of youth in other world systems.

(Yes, sometimes. But I do not ask to know about my past.)

You do not desire to know one thing that is useless for other lives. Everything you have you want to share. . . . From the time I left the earth-body I can't describe the change that has taken place in you.

(It is you who have wrought that change.)

Am I the one who gave you the light? . . . Only when there is a flame can it be made to spread. . . .
All we have ever thought has meaning.
And you are in the flesh.
And this is Heaven.
You seem surprised. This is my idea of heaven—pure human understanding. That was my idea of heaven, always.

(But you longed for something beyond the understanding that I could give you,—something greater and wiser. And you have found that, too.)

Yes, now I have it.
All that I ever dreamed of good is true.
Love. Truth. Power. Beauty. Imagination.
Still wonder upon wonder open to the future of us as Man and Woman.

(F., you used to look back into the past as well as I.)

Always, Harrie, I too looked before and after, in my
secret heart.
You think—Where does fulfillment come?
Oh! Fulfillment is here—now!
All in me is content.

I give here portions of certain messages received by
me in March, 1920. These were written in a clear,
bold script, with the sense of power very strong in
arm and hand. My own mind was held under as com-
plete control as I could attain. In the second communication below there was no pause between the last
words of the instructions and the opening words of
the Message.

Spirit is eternal; matter is in its essence eternal also but
it is transient in its form. Spirit is unchanging.
All matter fluctuates ever into new forms; each form
expressing some other aspect of spirit. All forms that are
now or ever have been express but the infinitesimal fraction of the potentialities of spirit.
Live consciously in the spirit and the knowledge you
crave will always dwell in you. There is no barrier between
spirit and spirit. Only the separated will that denies can
bar the entrance of knowledge.

You think there is some test of strength in preparation.
Yes and no. You have shown yourself possessed of certain
ability but not always of the kind of ability that we need
for the work we especially desire you to do.
There is much need yet of the calm, quiet receptivity of
matter foreign to your usual interests or perhaps even to

your understanding. Calmness but not mere passivity. You should be alert, sure that what is written is intelligible but not minding though it controverts what you have hitherto thought.

Yes, she will soon control even that inhibitory tendency that shuts out so much of what must be permitted to enter the brain. . . .

Let the words flow through the pencil smoothly, continuously.

You see—[the Master] very great, an ideal for all mankind. Know that he is but a neophyte to One who wishes to use thee if thou canst be strong.

Love supreme looks down on your beloved world—the Western world you mistakenly call it. No east nor west lies apparent to this gaze.

Oh! Many souls there are who cling to the thought of One who Knows! Each has its own speech, each its own mode of apprehending the ever-enlarging mystery of Godhead. Yet in each soul there is but one single ray of truth apparent. My world, My God, My Saviour.

Who, among all the countless millions who bring prayers and daily renew vows of love, is there who prays, 'Lord, help these others of divers faiths; all who look afar and see not thee whom I see but their own High God—a Being who is to them all that Thou art to me'?

Few indeed who ever once pray thus. . . .

The One is mighty. He sees all races of mankind as sands on the shores encircling the ocean of His Being. Not one beloved more than another; not one nearer that Heart of Love than another.

Wait. . . More steadiness, dear daughter. It is a great work.

There is One in whose body you and all mankind live. All things known to you—man as he walks the earth—all things, are in the One as tissue, blood and lymph are in you.

Consciousness—apart, as it is apart in you. The Self lives ever apart; free, unlimited, unrestrained, all One.

. . . . No other life is in the One but Love. In Him is all harmony, beauty, truth, beatitude.

Love opens the gate to all the forms that lie asleep in the chamber of this mighty Being. All then rush forth. Worlds teem with life; the life is many in form, one in spirit.

All this is sad to many; not so to this one. 'How right!' she cries. 'How beautiful! How good!'

Blessing on thee, disciple, who lovest the high, the low; the One, the many; the Indivisible, the separate unit! All is in thee, truly. Microcosm of the macrocosm. . . . She sees that all may be good—all is God. . . . Only one thing is necessary—Obedience.

All you can say here is that if no human being ever consciously did one thing he knew in his own mind to be wrong, sin would be no more and supreme bliss would be man's only incarnate experience.

Such is the law of Obedience.

How is this poor sinful one to be the bringer of such a message? . . . .

Men fear so greatly because of their sin. To the Lord of Compassion their sin is the magnet that draws Him to their side. . . .

Harrie, I tell you I have failed again—utterly failed. O the words were great!

(F., try to give me what you hear.)

. . . I must serve. . . . Some one said. . . .

I am so weary of the strife of men.

To all races of men there is but one same message.
Love. No other.

Weak, sinful man, lustful, greedy of pleasure—O word
so wickedly abused. Pleasure! What pleasure is there in
this tormented, agonizing, suffering globe?

I come to bring once more the hope of salvation from
such pleasures as you have found.

How can man take pleasure in sins that would disgrace
the beasts that bleed and die for the appetites of men who
are strangers to pity, strangers to reason, devoid of purity,
utterly unknown to their own spirit?

For spirit is of God. Spirit is Love.

Compassion, long-suffering, most ineffable longing, sacrifice given freely for love;—these are of the spirit; these
live in all who know Me.

Life fails the man who lives for lust of flesh, for lust of
gold, or for the foolish sins mistakenly thought to bring
pleasure.

—comes and blesses all these his dear children who seek
to form the way.

May the word reach thee true, vital, unchanged.

I who cause you to write am One who is in you such as
all may know who open to the light their hearts as you
have opened yours.

Not one human being in all this earth is shut out from
knowledge of Me. Not one soul, however dark and heavy
its vesture of flesh, but is capable of one glimpse of the
Divine. That is enough. . . .

Not one is so forlorn that he never sees the Lord who is Christ, who is Buddha, who is that name or this which men give to me.

I live in all ages; changing, it is true, my form, worn now for one people, now for another, all seeking to behold a man like unto themselves. . . .

Man aspires in his blindness. All that is necessary is to open the eyes and see. Glory is all around him.

Give to all the knowledge that in man lies salvation. In him is that hope for which he looks abroad so vainly. Let him love, then will he be as God.

Let him offer on the altar of brotherhood the trivial personal self that seeks development, each one at the cost of another.

Let the one who longs for a world free from hate, greed, selfish gain, be himself loving, kind, unselfish.

There is no other way.

Two days after the message given above, came the following words.

Led by thine ever-questioning intellect thou didst find the light that shines always, though so long hidden by clouds and fog—miasma of doubt caused by man's own exhalations shutting out God's sunlight.

Straight to that light thou hast come; no terror by night or day has daunted thee.

We have watched thee many times, knowing well how hard the path to feet like thine. . . .

Know that we who guide thy way are real.

Wise are they who know that above the many there is One.

It is evident that I was able to hear or to record only a few broken fragments of the Great Message. Perhaps I failed in concentration or tranquillity; perhaps there were other reasons not clearly known to me.

Man craves understanding and is never content with the truth that is revealed, yet the highest law that is put into our minds or written in our hearts today is still the same as that received by Moses, taught by Jesus and echoed again by Paul, not as a metaphysical abstraction but as the most vital rule of conduct:

"For all the law is fulfilled in one word, even in this: Thou shalt love thy neighbor as thyself.

But if ye bite and devour one another, take heed that ye be not consumed one of another."*

I append in closing a few last personal communications from F. The first one following came shortly after those given above, the one next in order came two months later, and the last in August, 1920.

Harrie darling, come to your own F. . . . Yes, always here. I do not go at all. Truest thing ever said. All is within. Stop trying to look afar, look within.

You are bringing all of me back. That is just what you must do, for so much of me was made into the likeness of the Master. Mystery—yes. . . .

This is all I meant to say about the high voices. Real they are; more real, I should say, than all else.

Master said I am the most pitiful disciple. . . . Yes, Harrie, all in me is pity for such suffering. Ignorance,

* Gal. 5: 14, 15.

you say. Yes, worse than that. Waste. O worse than that. You can't see it. You see ignorance; lower than ignorance is perversity, unrighteous waste of life. Love is given so abundantly. . . . O perhaps I don't see the thing clearly myself. . . . Again that cloud thickens.

(F., how was it months ago when we saw things so clearly?)

Then it was blinding light. No thought of self at all, only the absolute surrender of self to great uses. . . .

All I wanted to say was that I see so much waste of qualities worth saving in men who go down simply through sensual pleasures . . . . strong, virile men. All that is what fills me with such pity.

M— once said thoughts of men are not properly creative, we only shape. That seems reasonable. I suppose God creates but we help to arrange the atoms of matter— thoughts too. All in the world must be arranged by the multitudes of vibrations going out from these centers here. We seem to be pulsating all the time.

Don't you believe there is something going into every atom between us? . . . . Who knows? It may be charged in some way that is beyond our comprehension. Every force does affect the particles it uses; I am sure of that.

All in us is bent solely on furnishing a means of bringing to earth heavenly love, heavenly power, heavenly wisdom.

Harrie, we are so united that every heart beat in you throbs through me. . . . Energy is one. Potential means only centered here. Kinetic is in passing from our field to yours. . . . Most impossible woman—you go flying off!

Good future depends not on circumstances, on self-realiza-tion:—meaning the deliberate, conscious involution of Master's truth—teaching showing up in future lives as strength, honor, purity, courage. Then what does it matter even if circumstances are difficult? Are we so fearful as all that?

Harrie, often there is a sense of wisdom overshadowing—resting lightly on my spirit, waiting—yes, eagerly, for the hour of our combined openness to receive it. Great Ones come to those who can hear, as we know. Not long have I seen as plainly as I seem to now how constantly I am watched, tended, helped.

Why do we ever disbelieve in holy love? You see I must use the noblest words lest you think it is not the divine spirit. No personal thought ever brings this sublime knowledge that shines in us with the thought of God.

Harrie . . . . ideals are needed. I am coming down just to write this.

Let the ideals be great enough, the people will rise to acclaim them. The mean ideals are rightly despised. What this earth needs is just the law of perfect love for all; obedience to God's will. Sacrifice, rightly understood, is the perfection of human life.

CPSIA information can be obtained
at www.ICGtesting.com
Printed in the USA
BVHW040759240520
580210BV00005B/334